Love Is a Ghost Thing

Casey Mensing

PublishAmerica
Baltimore

ISBN: 1-60610-956-1
PUBLISHED BY PUBLISHAMERICA, LLLP
www.publishamerica.com
Baltimore

Printed in the United States of America

For my parents

LOVE IS A GHOST THING

Where should I put my eyes in this moment?

The rain outside falls gentle,
sonata
Your voice resounds,
trying to stop something that is dying

Your scent lingers in the breeze on the dark side of
the road
I return to see if you've risen above the flames
In the invisible cathedral you demanded charity
Ashes and blues in place of salt and sand
I listened to your voice pass through night

into broken light

Walking cheap gin forced you into a life of black outs
Mornings became weary tunes
My image became your other half, the night you
first took of your dress

Midnight became the moment of mysteries and
miracles

Quickened pulses
Until the sun rose over the rooftops

Darkness and magic falling into servitude
before any revelations

Those moments...
A mural painted on bed sheets
Decays in garbage grave

I went West with thought
Undecided in my intentions
Returned and found you with a new lover beside

The good-bye ripped through me like a desperate
bullet

Love is neither fantasy nor reality
It is the frozen moment of electro-shock
Thunder rolling over memories and genuflecting
ghosts

TELL ME LIES

The liaisons become more dangerous.
Our words are no more than clouds
given the importance of bones.

Falsehoods smelling of opulence and infertility
are considered divine reasoning.

In the distance,
there are ten twinkling lights all wishing
they were something else.

Together we could pretend the mountains are the
forests
the forests the mountains.

Neither of us enjoy impeding the progress of
illusions.

The I of the saga
is a virtuous bargain
compared to the sinuous savior of past revelations.

ADMIT INTO THIS ROOM

Admit into this room
the silence that is passing as all goes black.
I have traveled roads that lead from town to city
with eyes of dusk and misunderstanding.

Admit into this room
the night that seems infinite.
All stars, a prayer, long forgotten.

Admit into this room
the ghost of lost loves so I might be comforted by them
again.
I am vision without sound.

INTERSECTION

I watch the traffic
Cars and trucks
I watch the passenger side
doors become moving museums

glimpse
fragment
single still

memory or dream

man on the corner
broken teeth
stubble
sings ballads of the good times
when there was hope in every home.

ADMISSIONS AND REVELATIONS

Wine and water. Born under a desire sign. Feeling epic, like a three page scar.

Too high for longevity. Stars in my eyes. Fangs from seven days passed in my heel. The nights are mine.

Wasted on self esteem. Everywhere is nowhere. I can't see the smile, I thought I'd always remember.

The women of now, want to revel in your sex like the boys of the past. With heart I pulled you near. Lost myself.

Black and white photos. You, I, bed, wine. It's hard to forget the flecks of sun in your eyes.

Glances across a room. A smile seemingly sincere. Lying next to woman feigning love. How many versions of me are there on this night?

Knee deep and high. Making no sound. I'd turn my back on all of it for a moment with you. I'm a shadow.

Everyone I thought was dead is preventing me from reaching you.

CIRCUS OF SAINTS

Falling through the mirror in to the abyss. Ashes of salvation split my brow. Ears fill with the Spain of gypsies. Eyes watch water lap a swollen belly. Sudden birth. Sudden memory loss.

An Indonesian angel hovers above. Words descend from her burning lips like an exorcism prayer. My thoughts are a parable of broken limbs and celebrity razors. Moments of dry mating frozen in time.

Pursuing the majestic and fertile, the insatiable, wild with hallucinations. I plunge my fingers into paradise, sending angels into flight. The star that struggles to survive the dawn illuminates the poem. Smoke turns it into a lament. Crosses along the highway into a supplication.

I grieve for what took flight. Never again to descend. Holy innocent. Daughters of Joan of the Stake. Reduced to crimson cheeked harlots in the circus of saints.

AS IS

She walks alone. Moon close behind.

She burned away all traces of herself. Entombed the ashes in a bottle. Unbuttoned the boundaries. Rejoiced in the scattered explosions, tricks of lights.

Conquests became insignificant trophies. Her magic became an elegy.

Sun brought his daughter home. Replaced her opaque eyes with stars that comfort the midnight's lost.

LOVE POEM

I'm trying to forget
the taste of her that came with each kiss

stale smoke, quiet desperation

I'm trying to forget
how she clung to me for warmth

clung to me to fill the void

I wonder how she felt
the next morning

when she realized
I was hollow inside

TRANSGRESSIONS IN TIME

Some days advance backwards. Beauty is only matched by the music of solitude. Though one seems more than the less, neither are consolation.

Swayed by my gullibility. Nothing but shadows to rely on. Fading memories in hand. A cross nailed through the bone.

The moon and you, here, gone, watch me smoke my last of the night and I start believing I'm not alone.

Twenty miles from a new road. The heat licks my lips like a Saturday night drunk girl. Leaves at my feet. Limbs cast shadows like skeletal fingers. Perception clouds itself in obsession.

Voices tangle like limbs. The flowers roar as they are resurrected from winter's tomb. Repulsing those who only want to see death. The day is the night is the day.

NOTHING LIKE SMOKE

Relinquished the moon. Invented dreams. Been seduced by the perfumes of princesses. Lifted veils from the eyes of the dead. My world is limitless.

The stars share their affliction. Their lights collision with my eyes. What separates us in death and minutes?

I don't recoil from the way I began. From outstretched arms or smoky groans. New affection is felt. Dreams feel like memories. Realizations of a past life. A shadow around my neck. I see tulips laid to waste. Ancient pain of the East. Witness avoiding strangulation. Stripped of all but light. Surrounded by a whirlwind of smoke. Keen eyes of youth disappear.

Illumination crosses the threshold.

HERE

On the tips of my fingers
there are nothing but stars

Here, people pray
Give thanks
Here, new invocations are born
The real and unreal
bleed
into one another

Here, we watch life unfold
Eyes rolling back into heads
as we dive into the sea

As before
I awaken alone
sand clinging to skin
Mind and eyes opened to the night
A new creed on my tongue
All around, silence
Then waves crash

Above is a starry night
as envisioned by
Van Gogh

AND I WISH

Across shiny beer taps I spy
those playful eyes
that send me swirling.

My mind tips over
leaving me to play the game with subtle glances.
In secrecy I scribble silent dreams about your smile
but all words are in vain.

And I wish...
To feel lips swell with passion kiss.
To feel nipple grow under tongue touch.
To run fingers along soft love lips,
piercing sex center with prick-heart.
Arms and legs tangled, wrapped around,
waist...chest...neck.

All nerve endings on edge...

Anticipating

FIRST DAY OF SUMMER

Outside is an oven
Smell of winter juniper is a memory.

A sense of lightning and illusions
of violence and foreign countenances
of flames becoming enlightenment.

Disengaged from impurity
In dreams we are smoke
Suffocating others with our ethereal nature

Modernist heights are now patterns on neck ties
Nooses are still plain and rough like a farmer's
hands

A river needs momentum to serve it's destiny

Who filled the afternoon rain with secrets?
Who filled the garden with nocturnal rage?

We fear bones, strong or deformed
Gnaw on them, now that our sense of shame is
gone.

SPIRIT IN PRISON

Scarlet and bone
Breath again provides me with life

Sun burns low
Dimmer...dimmer...
gone.

Somewhere dark night exists and the illusions I
dream are real.
I fear thief time more than the devil himself.
Miracles exist all around but ignorance acts as a
cancer of the eye, blinding us.
A prayer of sexual desire is used to invoke
something lost inside.
Conviction is thrown against the mute hills.
Faith confesses to the deaf trees.
Prayer becomes falling tears, that weigh down flowers.
Broken fingers try to sign the symbols of sin.
Again the horizon becomes alive and inflamed.
Heart breaks because of the passivity of grace.
The dreamer is left to dwell.

KEY TO THE SHRINE

Plagued by self-created delusions
Pierced by metaphors
Blessed and debunked
Pregnant with ideas
Reduced to dreamed outbursts

Smashed glass

First night of escape
The discovery of sin
Convinced there is no death
Only sleep

SKIN REVEALS

Unmasked hours. Fate reveals itself.
Where are the glasses?
The bottle we held up to the moon?

Broken on your floor!

Spring purple sky outside.
I rejoice because your body is smooth

All knowing

Beneath mine

LEAVING

buildings have ears
prophets of night share their crooked insight

the rhythm is blue and insurmountable
coming of day brings distress

there are murderous words floating above us
hushed tones of a child's prayer echo in my head

my dreams contain burning eyelids
mirrors and windows wail over their own broken
glass

dead radio waves are noxious
my shirt is stained with the words spit upon it

yours is a switchblade tongue
mine, a welcoming chest

ours, was a bed of riddles

NIGHT IN THE TRAP

The beer is cheap. American.
The night is tawdry. American.
Time moves like quicksilver
The past yells into the ear of the future
"What is being?"
"What is believing?"

BEYOND...

Lick the eye with love
Follow with a long silence
Step into the void
Dream it all again
We're composed of white noise
Midnight is without dimensions
The center is breath
Flesh a mere memory
Bones now dust
Spirit becomes unchained and all seeing
Infinity for a few precious seconds

ROOTLESS

Tried by fire
Resurrected in water

To HER I write riddles revealing my childish contempt

Lost love like a falling star

She is on the porch of a different house waiting to hear
my vows

I am without shape
Impermanent thoughts leave my mouth
Grief is the only certainty

I've been baptized twice
Neither time did I close my eyes or think to shout

ESCAPE

A decade and change
What to remember?
What to forget ?

A place that more resembles an abortion of space
than a city or place

Only forward and moving
Conscious or comatose I take it all in
Back there,
there was no chance to win

FAREWELL TO BELLS

Her smile reminds me of a rainy night, Nashville
skyline.

I loved all the suggestive girls on the deck of cards
she played.

Jealousy would come and go with eyes and
utterances.

The moon full, night air thick, heavy.
I return to the sea.
Shadow and sand cast.
Imbued with water's song.

Words for a girl with change on her floor.
Barefoot and pregnant on her front porch.

Whitman resting on her belly.

When next I see her,
she'll have a child in her arms,
as sunlight pours through my fingers.

THE BEAUTIFUL WORLD IS WEIGHED DOWN BY GRIEF

On the left side of Autumn, past the indulgence of the setting sun, I wander streets that are lined with disagreements, singing alternate endings to forgotten songs.

Accidents bleed into mythology. I shake my head at the ridiculous forms passing from eyes, to mind, until invisible.

Curses are agendas worth hiding from.

The hands of the clock move with subtle obedience. I am magnanimity with a toothless grin. Keeper of the last seat on the carousel.

In the wake of fear and invisible people, I sink into the dark womb of mother sea.

SHE SAYS SHE'S AN ACTRESS

Prisoner of abandonment. Child without shooting stars.

Silk screen and smoke empire. Walking through a citadel on fire. Becoming the ripe fruit of the smug.

Contained within you are a thousand deep night stars, shielding you from the blunt and ruthless examiners without decency.

Recite through lips of Babylon, blessings for the men with silvery tongues. Seduce the mute on the street. Turn ashen, the million faces like yours.

Sun always cast a weary light as your soul passes through the narrow slit of an eye.

When men come with their metaphors and honest deformities, lay your trembling hand upon their imaginations. Alleviate them of the atrocity of their empty mouths.

When broken glass cuts causing separation, place upon countenance the mask that will sustain you.

FOOL OF LOVE STREET

Heaven is stars and impetuous voices.

Heart a temper all its own

Carnal skull is full of lover's memories
Lust, demands spring must come before the dawn

Missionary times are long past
Awkwardness, a flash of light
Tonight, only you and the moon rage
Darkness, driving you to become Hamlet at sanity's
edge.

She is a girl of different melancholy
No solid eye to return your gaze.

Heart, teeth, soul, and bones are your offerings to
her
In return she must love you and remove her mask

RAIN AND LOSS

Lies are innocent when laced with moonlight.

Your body is my sole narcotic.
Toes to thighs. Hips to eyes.
I linger.

In lost hours we count planes as shooting stars.
Planets become reminders of lovers that left without
a farewell kiss.

Exchanging infinity for small talk and a night to not be
alone.
This bed is now a foreign country and I can't
understand my lover's tongue.

A DREAM THAT WALKED THROUGH

Snakes slip through fingers. Bedside carnations wilt. Tree's fruit falls passively.

Your heart is now tears, soon to be a sea.

Flashes of childhood. Sounds of a town with blue-eyed dreams.

Traces of soil on your tongue. Tranquility. Sidewalk scars. River streets. Compassion lost and found. The dream has been derailed. Held captive. Crosses marking graves are flames.

Day draws its pale eyes closed.

FIRST DESIRE

Welcoming night.
Laying rose petals at the gypsy girl's feet.
The wind and violin. Nothing more. Support her
dance.
Sorrowful and pure.
The circus is populated by celestial forms
Born of the dancer's ecstasy
Immortality the sum of her parts.

FIRST FEVER

Two lives into you. Reaching. Stroking. Flesh walls
collapse into one another.

Cruelty opened the wound that allowed the raven
to nest

Like a child you lay struggling. Pure morning snow
as your backdrop.

I should have been gentler
I was a boy with a new crown

New found mysticism. Leaving for a time the
confines.

You were only half a moon

A white oleander crushed
in the palm of my hand.

BEING AND IMAGE

Hindu goddesses walk the shore. Hair of silk and ink. Saris of gold and red. Small brown feet tickled by the sea.

High tide waves crash, untangling my mind. I idealize, romanticize, sanctify moon and her stars, water and sand.

Goddesses of the shore.

Here to escape the sameness of the city conversations that echo the past.
Naked, mere flesh and bone, penetrating surf and sea. Diving for pirate gold, mermaids, rising up again.
The breath of life.

Beyond purity, a city is stretched to its limits.
Over wrought and servicing the dead.
I am the abyss and heavens.
Flora and Fauna.
Being and image.

3

You were a trinity
One of flesh. Two of shadows.

Long lost in paranoia, Zen-like moments, dreaming only of suffering.

Naked seeking atonement. Calling the evidence of crimes coincidence. The flames will reach even the most tender of hearts. Debts will be collected by idiots and whores.

They way you were lost, is the way you'll be found. In the shallows of the river, memories will be drowned.

Ascension promised, is now delivered.

PERFECT IMAGE REARRANGED

I create patterns and dreams out of the faces in the
windows I pass

The time has come to visit the ghosts of old illusions

One way streets

Genuflecting to the ones that know but never
speak
The void becomes a body. Dreams become
shadows.
The visions and lamentations of messy breeding
I try writing postcards to your delicate stars, velvet
folds
Love and despair

Eyes placed in a sleeping man's mouth
The nights lengthen, becoming defenseless
Softer are the lies, the parables of my drunken
tongue
I am numb
Transitional inside

Sun peeks through the blinds, burning away
dreams, last night
No reason to count notches on bed post or spine

Been the distance. There are two hearts interwoven
with mine
Choking on counterfeit narcissism
The noiseless ledge

Broken silences. Lost on streets of revolution.
Wandering through diamond florescence
Her requiems reach ears
First love, first blood is now a woman laden with
memories

No reason to grieve in silver night

Smoke ties itself up in your hair
I'm high on the smell of small town air
We sit listening to the words the fire preaches
Lingering

Pawing a rosary, my head is like a burnt match
Faces of forever. Moon swells beyond reasoning
Discordant music. Every nerve a prayer. Logic is
useless

A creator adoring the fingers of a destroyer.
Tomorrow is as vague and distorted as the heavens
My eyes thc only thread to the physical world, are
still full of flowers. My chest full of stars. Whole
constellations.

SUNDOWN'S FINISH

Smoke finds the flame as my harmonica cries a somber tune to your name.

Lost in the you in front of me and the one of another time
Reaching for the melted sunlight in your eyes as a thousand blackbirds wait at the horizon, because the stars fade there.

From under cigarette smoke rising, dark circles around my eyes ask the question my voice cannot.

What is it you're thinking as my lips press into the fire of your skin?

PARANOIA WALTZ

Bridges burned before I could cross. Songs of flame and illumination. Smoke and vanishing kisses. Silence swallows thunder. Beneath black tulips lovers are sleeping.

All roads are paved with bone. This is the heartache of the mothers that brought the ribs and femurs I walk upon into the world.

Streets narrow, getting tighter. Vacant eyes looking into windows searching for a story to tell. Moving through cultures in order to find home.

Each living angel wiser than the next. Each speaks of the promise that was made. The melody of crying echoes through the gardens and the years.

M

The chatter
chatter

repetition of words
that rhyme with leaves

Decided
Deserted
I wish not to be found again

Finally

Don't think about
Smoke and rain

Don't think about
Why not

Let those days
Stray away

WESTERN NIGHT

Four on the road. Rolling over bones. Searching for something that feels like home.

I slide through loneliness and stars, pockets of infinity, out of reach.

The black hills are rising above, the forest that hides, a lifetime of forgotten eyes.

Succumbing to fever and painted faces. Distant wails of a past life. Paralyzed by apologies.

Things said beneath the leaves.

NO END OF TOMORROW

Deformed, deaf, dumb, driven by the unseen, rebellious heart.

In the garden, angels with tongues of fire, speak of their immortality.

Words bathed in honey and violence. Enraged, trying to break their chains, until everything is dead.

Each lashing and wound, each moment of eyes and utterances, my heart becomes tender.

Grief unlike any other.

How grim, being something, that cannot die.

LIGHT OF SUBMISSION

In a room of lace and dusty window sills, you await
your Christ's absolution. Lit by the things that
steal from you, a hymn coils around your mind that
no one can hear.

I unfurl in late night creations. Long eyes glance.
Love is a simple French song.

Obsessed with love's poverty, together we fear
being born, or slowly dying.

Speak to me in broken silence of skeletons in your
closet. Of broken hearts. Of the mirrors you hide, in
penetrable darkness.

Hallow hands knock. Angel feathers float like
forgotten words at resurrection's door. Outside,
beauty prays beside railroad tracks. I dream of the
moon as your naked form clings to me.

REAL?

Broken. Head full of excess. Crossing blackened waters. Distant lights streaming.

In a nowhere room. Lost within myself. Her bare skin is sliding against mine.

She and I. Lingering. Touch. Penetration. Orgasm. Real?

Eyes into eyes. Stare. Searching for connection. Promises. Hips align. Pleasure.

Left and Right. Sides decided. Compromise. Phantom bond. Lost in sleep.

TENDER IS THE NIGHT

Daisies and the eastern sun used to be enough.
What's left to get you through?

You can no longer hide behind whispers and
watery eyes.
You traded all your flowers for Jamaican rum

Out on the street you walked, drunkard's eyes in
your pocket, a Spaniard's hallucinations in your
shoe. Life's last sensation long past. Salvation all
that remains.

Everyone around me is still high. An ambulance
sighs.

The night outside is sticky and slow moving.
Nothing but restless dreams, faded memories.

The moon is half of itself.
I'm looking for words to say, what I should have
already said

It's hard to speak without a tongue.

I'm feeling like the back of an unread novel as I melt
into the night.
Staring out of the window
from which you
leapt.

IN THE DAYLIGHT

Quickly, memories trickle.
Van Gogh. Field. Blackbirds. Scattering. The end.
Time passes slowly. Endless mangroves before his
eyes. He wonders if any blackbirds will scatter.
Click. Crack.
His eyes fill with blackbirds.

NAKED NEEDS

Tongues seek out lips as the butterflies of July flutter and twist in the heat.

I kissed purpose and put lyric to bed. Swept up the glass of a broken window, from the fight that pays no resemblance to the memory.

Struck again by the river weepers. Trying to conceal my sadness from you. Trying to convince you I'm not delusional.

The circle is dust left clinging to our feet.
The whole is the harmony of two colors.
Which stand together.
Apart.
Intensifying.

LOVER OF SUN AND MOON

What's done in life, mingles with the blue light of death.

These four walls are anywhere, always.

Detached from future and past. Eroticism breaks apart the afternoon. I am hers when the moon is encircled by flames.

Her body is love torn, a canvas of scars and tattoos, places and lovers.

She wasn't always an open wound.

She was once worshiped. Then gave into wanton words of sun and moon.

She is a fire that burns, still singing the songs of the elements, dancing until the heathens believe.

TIME IS A STRAY BULLET

Time is a stray bullet.
A mute, recurring dream.

Humble storyteller, swallowed alive by the past,
stands before me with a star for a heart.

Morning breaks open with saved lives.
Last night was a thousand words, desires, that had
to be buried
in the blue-black-gray.

VICTORY OVER SWIMMERS

Everything before us, a geometric figure dissolving
in the acid of sunlight.

Salvaging the wreck of her soul.
Drinking in tears
Feasting on loss
Throwing no stones.

The sea devours a spirit.
Cries turn to mud in her throat as the wind whips
her sunset hair, dirty and dreaded.

We watch a black dog run across the waves,
convinced it is an illusion of the moon.

Nothing inside but promises of future phantom
kicks.
Years if the occasional backward glance.

SUSPENDED FROM THE SKY

Head filled with moths. Prophetic breath vanquished. Penitent beggar imagines a fallow paradise. Without remorse he scorches mansions and weapons because too many mothers are weary of death.

Ungrateful and bleeding beneath a sycamore, coated in the ashes of others, Cain, with hands of flaming flowers, knows a sexless temple propagates violence.

A sorrowful chronicler in another's guise, with a haggard expression around dim eyes.

A long whiskered sailor afraid of drowning in the dirt of his home town knows stars are nails to hang our dreams on.

Whose shadow is nothingness will be born again a mute.

There are those struck down. Those burdened by crowns. The arrogant prefer the dust that spills from the mouths of the arrogant.

Windows and doors are opened. New dead leave. What remains?

CURVE OF THE DAY

Sun is sinking to rest. Chasing oranges and purples until they slip through fingers.
Night is a labyrinth. Souls nursing secret fears as tarantulas crawl out of open mouths.
Feet amongst the sharks teeth. Staring at washed out mountains.
Snakes coiling up my spine.
It's harrowing to sleep through falling knowing nothing is at the bottom.
Dawn, the earth is damp. Birds sing from cypress branches. Loneliness moves into another day.
When the sun is at its highest,
earth is scorched,
wilderness is silent

HERO AS A SAD CLOWN

Matches burn like dead flowers. The lady who holds the world's pain is strangled by her own martyrdom. An outlaw fresh from salvation, having castrated the gallows, merges with morning.

Sun recalls his first love. Moon is a forsaken vessel. Night, dissipates into the bloody milk of morning. Fragrance of those remembered in an autumn rain.

Graveyards hold the secrets of our ancestry. Hiding truth. History of lovers not buried beside one another.

Death no longer seems miraculous, just a restless angel with a fruitless womb. Soaked in the sweat of a recurring nightmare. Proctoring over an endurance test. Handing out consolation prizes to the losers.

His world exists without silence.
An elegy without a hero.

VERGE OF MYSTERY

A backward glance.
Dilated pupils can no longer see the people I've revealed secrets to.
Tried to release, only to make myself a prisoner.

Forced confrontations. Lovers taken. Absorbed.

Neon wanderings. Singing shallow grave blues.
Returning to the well work road.

Struggling to be born again of the light.

SERPENT AND CLOWN

You are organless and slow moving. Real. Ready to be executed.

She is vacant. Always with the strand of a song in her head as she moves with opulence down the street.

When you collided, it was a reminder of your impotence and her bitterness.

Now you two share a bed
Capricorn and cancer
Lost in metaphors and needs
Time shaping your faces.

I NEVER KNEW SILENCE

I miss your knees
The sunshine that illuminated my path of self-
destruction

Your home has no room for me
Your bed is no longer a place for me to dream

We saw the end coming for miles
Strands that bound severed without words or
regards

I hear the song you sang when you were part of my time
I hear the words fade that let you down

Violin kissing elegant neck
Soft summer dress swaying across tops of knees
You're an unrealized Audrey H.

Your leaving created a silence that I had never
known
Nightly walks pass the hours
Every long street and forgotten alley I expect to find you
Stars in your hair
Moon in your chest.

WHOLE, IMAGINED

Velocity of creation. A masquerade of sun moon sea. Pregnant with ideas. Birthing stillborns. Wilderness is again illuminated. Stars belong to the Imagists. Nights glowing eyes have their own religion. They'll be here long after we're gone. Miracles have been prostituted. The visitation made absurd. Self delusion the only solution. No eyes to lie in the light.

Carbon monoxide. An embrace that liquefies the spine. Vision in a tongue that dances through falling skies. Syncopated prayer meeting. A dove casts hallucinations. Tigers are of snow and ice in jungles of moonlight.

Broken souls. Tongues of allegory and shadows. Silver lined sighs and pretense. Visions, stolen words. Refuge, hidden from our eyes. Flames are fixed and infinite. Bound as captive. Forsaken as prisoner. Angles envy the tongues of libertines.

Hymns are a string of words, like pearls, torn from the throat, as a prize for the divine.

Streets fall silent. Others sleep. I walk through these hours, seeking understanding and vengeance. Fighting the creeping blindness, the voices from last night. Headlights. Traffic lights. Trees. Concrete. No stars bleed through the pollution. The street preacher. The bible quotes. All comes to pass. Ashes to ashes. Back alleys of wild dogs, beer bottles. Girls in their knees. Musicians lost in syphilitic visions. This is the place of beginnings.

DEPARTING

Everything outside of myself is stained.
Fingers cut the dust. Window ledge becomes
patterns.
My decisions, testaments.

Time is marked by a change in colors
Attitude.
Every moment revealing splendor.

I step with madness down all night streets
I turn up the sun and moon until their light
becomes ecstasy
Drowning out the neon
Headlights, tail lights
until they become a series of dreams

Wondering what set the universe in motion
Reenacting my renaissance
All pain trapped in memories is dying
My imagination is devoured by sleep

The divine are tongueless
Murdered by man's translations

Memories are never the exact manifestations of the beautifully once was.

A magician's accusation.

A juggler's dream.

Grief becomes a prayer meeting.
Illuminations disguised as sun and moon.

Cunning, choking on guilt
Seducer, bleeding lust
They are amongst the dedicated with rapture in their eyes
waiting for the concubine to be burnt alive

A smile through the veil
Eccentric traffic in the corridor of time.

LOVE'S FORGOTTEN NAME

Quiet nights
Time passes like a breath
I get lost in reason's translation
Listening to the ageless river of love saying good-bye

I always open the door expecting to find
quicksilver eyes and missionary tongue
hands clutching the remains of a baby bird that
tried too soon to fly

Clearer now is my mind
as I peer into the darkness that surrounds
Smoke dancing through the winter air with
graceful sorrow

I am mute like the thought that sent me dreaming

A flower in a blue vase reminds me of love's forgotten
name

ADAGIO

Consuming alcohol. Nicotine eating me alive. Reciting various verses of the King of May. I desire to slide away.

From tongue leaps demise. The rain washes away forever and it is useless to lament dreams. Here there are no promises. And when the streets are barren, endless love is satisfied.

Loss of psychedelic virginity. Narrowly surviving the attack of that which wishes to drink my blood. Now I'm raw. Connection. The fall out of daylight. Just you and I alone, handcuffed in acid dream cells. Lessons on becoming... Undressing images of reality. Laughter comes from the doorway, a woman with words overflowing from her pocket, with a smile that's torn the heart out of lovers and a shadow that drifts with time.

Your myths depend upon you. Delirium is all too beautiful. Will another hour of life be enough? My black poems grow like strange flowers, that you've forgotten, leaving them in the mud with your freedom. My mind has been ploughed, made fertile again. I've bagged the abstract and am honored with a corpse's penny. I will release it when I am old and decadent, my spirit mutated. As I awaken from embryonic dreams, I find nothing is real. Vanity has caused my failure. Impatience has struck me on the ass like a wet towel.

There are innocent soldiers fighting a war against our senses and the clouds hang like nooses predicting a bitter end. Blinded by white nights, you rip the candy crucifix from my neck, and I spit priceless words into your face. You forced me to clump my love into lumps because it made me soft. Now the sweet wheel of my locomotive will embrace your throat.

Forgive me for my inaudible silence when your beauty entered the room. Forgive us Huck Finn, we know not of what we do. So quit throwing stones and reading from a bible that has been joint rolled. I will give you a thousand housebroken illuminations if you cease your distractions. Open your windows! Unlock your doors! There's a poetic renaissance outside.

Worship together all you sordid tongues of fire. Whisper symphonies as the sun screams beauty at the moon. Bare goddess of love, elaborates on these lustful games like a thousand knives in the back.

Johnny Nolan still has a patch on his ass. We are all exchanging roles with ease and the sky is always an orangish-brown, so I throw curses at it contemptibly. In 1961 death came at puberty for masturbating was a sin, sin, sin.

A portrait painted in the heart of man. Recollections of childhood immortality. A black sea from which all things are created. Posterity given with tenderness. Who are the spectators?
Who are the actors? I wish to drink up youth but am afraid I'll drown. It can no longer be resisted And poetry is nothing more than an impression. A series of shadows cast into seas And the angel in me is constantly shocking the few who think they know TRUTH.

I'm flipping through the thirty-third printing of someone's mind, their meditations in regards to...Tranquility. There is a love of phantoms within us all for they are all about us whispering, "I'm lonesome for my heroes". What does it mean? Exchanging sex for misery Dance enchanted whore queen.

Ravel's soundtrack. Your karma resolved. Your bleeding wounds beauty on my page. What a delicious thrill it is to be condemned.

I want to feel. To catch all the butterflies. All my lucid thoughts are still only a penny, though the price of dreams has increased. Inflation in the gentle abyss. Neon wilderness. My hands are on the pale rose and I'm looking for another way, anything but the same.

Nothing to hold on to. My lover's suffocate me, the words just fly from here to there, falling anonymously. Tiny invocations. It's much to quiet outside and I don't know if the dead are cursing, praying, or sighing with relief. I'm not sure if I can be that way. The new truth is as fraudulent as the past's.

I wrote my dreams on spring leaves watched them change and die. What time is it in heaven? Are they waiting for me and my angels to die? Giving life to poison flowers that are given in love, meditated upon, saved for a lifetime. Submissive in Sutras and dirty dreams. Blinded immortality, then shot in the back. I gave away death on a highway, spewed expectations upon floral shroud and asked superheroes to by merciful and entertain.

Nothing seems like it used to. I secretly long for thorns. Poison trees of Blake. Ravens of Poe. Drunken boats of Rimbaud.

I've read the catalogs of the soul that are full of battered meat. In response I throw to the heavens vague words with meanings that are impossible to discover.

Sitting in my own shadow, laughing in the face of tragedy, the days falling through me. I dream of being emblazoned upon imagination but there's nothing but uncertainty. And things are the way they are because it took forever to see the blood. I am the hero and villain of my own dreams (the only one willing to court the muse).

I suffer in dreams, but all is well. I strip the clothes off the open air. I'm left feeling a curious sensitivity towards believers. Beasts dance Yin and Yang to ragtime jazz confessions and cum on their thighs. Another passes go with no money in hand. Now they have a lot they can't tell you. The same silences are repeated Your bitterness is undeniable. I've eaten away the sweet layers of myself and mine, painted your eyes upon the wall hoping for a prophecy. I sucker-punched your napalm kiss with mastorbatory fist. Slyly, I winked and let the universe go on. Then tragedy jumped because tragedy was surprised. And I kissed the ring finger of Whitman to ensure prophesy. Read the rules of the contest, cried in despair. The agony of no real winner.

How will it feel when death is upon me? Will I be able to fill the gaps? Scribbling and smiling as all that is about me disappears. And no long winded good-byes, for I have triumphed. My poetry illustrates this feat. As do the death threats I never sent. And the morphine I injected with pure genius in order to abstract. With eyes opening, chalk one up for poetry, charity, imperfection.

Ghost tongue speaks unquestionable truth. These varying explanations of why things are the way

they are have caused my mind to wander. I pull a
new name out of a hole in the ground, search for
diamonds amongst the litter of words, and it feels
good, though flesh has again made a fool. And it all
must pass through my minds eye. For I am a saint.
A clown. A man making himself a beast, to escape
the pain of being a man.

he thinks like a king

SUCKERPUNCH

"Give me another drink and maybe they won't notice that I was allowed life again. And again they'll have that look of surprise—that panic attack—as fury spits forth from my eyes!"

No one knows everything, despite the twisted nature of God's sense of humor. These horrors have left me feeling stupid and lonely, and I find myself looking through the personal ads for someone I can pass through—much like the days that have come and gone in no certain order, though I end up in a different place in the end. I feel distant and this has rendered me emotionally useless to all but a select few, all of whom wander long streets in southeast Asia, looking for the man they call Nashville. So I still wait for them, or Nashville, or the delivery of a black and white TV that's typewriter compatible.

Strangers go by again. Pretending to be happy. Pretending to be alive. But they are anxious and uncertain. It's lead to sleepless nights, cigarette punching, and face-stealing in the name of happiness. I say to them, "Manipulate all you can

73

while you can, because someday someone's going to try to take you over and your only defense is song and dance or wonderful breasts and you, my dear sainted friend, have neither. So grow a beard and paint your toenails, become a pop star for the deaf and dumb and never mind the bastards, because they're God's favorites...

My emotional shin is thin and I'll never show you anything. My paranoid hallucinations were right about everything. "Appeasement" is too strong of a word and "pity" might be used too much as an excuse for actions. No one really cares how many people live inside you, as long as all of them give in to sly demands.

I wish all the people here would take someone home with them tonight and color naked with them. Or go battle someone, anyone, but me—I'm still patiently waiting.

I see all the things I think of, and, at times, I just want to hug the night with my invisible arms and wait for it to spit me back out until I'm the last one left.

How am I supposed to concentrate on that which is not free form? The absolution of form gives us 1950. Some might say that joy comes in the form of nothing attainable and the LMNOP of oxygen intake caused Alexander the Great respiratory problems. Of course, I couldn't care less about those claiming to be prophetic.

Did you know that the meek would fight back? Regardless of your vision, regardless of continuity, and mistaken assassinations, debating the obscene is a dream. And the gentle nightmare brings it all together in less than a thousand miles. Once again, there are rumors of Nashville, our returning hero, he's got all he needs and will never fall, despite the rumors of his subtle inability. And in these crossroad times, a man asks for torture and we give him tickets to thirty years ago.

Who wants to go back to where they came from? The obvious reasons as to why it might be best are of no concern as the night turns from black and white into inside out.

I'm the fool. I've given more than I should have. Shown more than I should have. Vanity is patiently waiting for heartache. I forget to forget the things that need to be forgotten but the conversation between me and myself never ceases to exist.

The bullets that riddled the body have left us separate but equal. The radio plays companion pieces to go with a symphony of heartache no one has ever heard. I try to steady myself. Ready myself to speak my mind, no matter what the ghosts I clutch in my hand have to say about the reality that haunts them this and every other night. And my thoughts are not well. Self involved—absorbed—playful in their ingenuity—realistic in their dimension. There goes the change and it rains again. Long ago, I readily gave up my fortune for revelations.

Does your car, make noises of salvation when you drive through small towns? I guess I need to talk to someone without having to make a phone call. The ballads swirling in my mind, remind me of another day when it was horses in the streets and everything felt lukewarm and curiosity didn't exist because God hadn't yet invented it. And dreams made people happy and no one knew the word sorry but perfectionists and the shadow players. Up hills we walked through snow searching for shame because it seemed silly to whip ourselves without it. This is how it was and would still be if people would have stopped wasting their lives on romantic notions and apostrophes. So doubt me not! The quotation marks have no hold on Tom Foolery or the clever pet names he has for friends, lovers, and heretics.

There's a cold front moving in and life seems to stop without a thought. Only a tie-in, a thread in nightmares plot for the sake of a TV movie. And the song of freedom is stuck in the throat of the masses!

ASPECTS IN SILHOUETTE

There is no magnetism in the air at 2 am. The driver's wasted and I'm much the same.

The ecstasy is brought to you by a Frenchman in drag. Amusement—the language used.

America is gaining surety again. Controversy has become the clown prince. Truth and happiness have become musicals. Darkness is still art. And the same dream ends. The station tuned to the same channel.

Killers of the past, resurrected for the sake of entertainment. Shadow beliefs set before our feet. A second-rate strip show. A drink sipped, swallowed. The future is blue love and the return of wife swapping.

I have eaten too many mornings. Elaborated on too many thoughts. The old self is resurrected, hoping for tranquility. The book closes. My bag is packed, full of all the things I've seen. The salvation car will take me as far as I need to be.

I've taken to riding the rolling thunder. Found solace in ex-patriots and forty-year-old photographs. Evidence is in lies.

Half-sick guitars and blessings aged with time. Nothing left to mourn for but glory's speeding train.

The animal has become abstract. Moments bagged properly, then given a Viking funeral. Writing lines, she deserves to have written about HER. It all comes in. It all goes out.

I want to take that wall that left tears in my eyes to see the world.

Every thing's plucked from my pride. Hand in hand, Delilah and I walk, trying to no longer change the course of the universe.

Chain smoking like a virgin. Pretty Pop Princess, known as Pseudo-Lolita, is suffering from the um's and her mouth is quite dry. She's in need of a fix but none of the drugs she knows work. This doesn't matter to me. My candles burn down the same. I've discovered secrets that no one can discuss. I'm just trying to keep the dogs at bay.

Getting high on love found. But the ghosts are still following me. The nightmares of Indian summers. The blues of Lightin' Hopkins. Everything in between. The teeth are like aluminum when they clamp down.

Living in my clothes. Genius suffers from a barrage of rejection. And I ache for something just like a woman. I've been blessed, but not like the rest. My hallucinations and horoscopes hold true. Those wine bottle kaleidoscopes help pass the time. The faces of a million people pass before my eyes. Is there any place they're going to?

The roses taste like whiskey. Is there a tree in Mississippi that doesn't carry a reminder? The blood was never washed away from where the innocent lay slain.

Some people touch me. The driver says, "It's like finding a dirty foot in your pudding."

Times worth more than money. Terrible dreams are like sound bites that find their way into the closet. I awake unnerved. Remove the quotations from the wall. Across the way, the bedroom light stays on. Everyone thinks, but the thief gets beaten anyway.

The melancholy trumpet player finds the bottom. The winds reveal the future, by carrying the words of the past. I'm still grieving for the voice after the song is sung. It's easier to move on once the roots have given away.

Candy-cane colored skeletons. All the young girls hide their names. The downstairs woman runs into the darkness, and light paints her all the same either way. Everyday at 8am, she knocks on my door and begins screaming, "I have no sense!" I just always assumed she meant time. The guy who lives in the woods behind the KFC, always tells me she does this because of her fear of cartoons. I have no time to figure this out for myself. I have no intentions.

The dark had long since begun. Dawn is fighting to be born. The religion of handcuffs and crawling out of windows is ceremoniously underway. And all I can do is grin in these moments of bathtub prostitution. I've made contact with someone who's hiding from what they don't know. Running from something that doesn't exist. But she'll never understand that her disposition is not my problem. My alcohol fogged eyes have nothing to do with her misfortune.

"Did the hemlock stop the burning desire or just leave you feeling blue? Are you tired of playing second fiddle to a Jesus type?" These are the questions I asked the driver at 7:33, after he claimed to have had a vision. His life has turned another corner and I'm just dreaming while I can.

Drunk, we charge like cowards in a bad western and hell will laugh at our fury. But we continue on with indifference—for we're in control of the chaos that is swirling about us and I've placed all my bets on the muse.

When I walked into the room, it smelled like sad imitation. A mess that will never be cleaned up. A thousand Muhammad Ali's feeling like the boy Cassius. Another child is lost to the savage bastards of propaganda. Buy me, I'll be your best friend, your lover, your spaceship to the moon and then I'll move on with a smile and a shuffle. Chaplin's got nothing on me.

There was once a time when anything could have happened. There was nothing to grieve and that was the key. And we all wondered what a good life was made of. Was it anything like little boys or girls? And for longer than a second at a time we all knew what we were, what we were made of, where we were going. Then nap time came, maybe some milk and cookies, a little coloring in the afternoon, creativity was promoted, nonconformity was for those lactose intolerant kids that drank juice from home. And right now, I've got nothing but patience for that which makes little sense because it's all gonna work out. This is an obvious prophecy. And it's not madness that's destroying the best minds of my generation, it's cowardly apathy—otherwise known as the damn foolish fear of FEELING.

I go back left. One hand has seen what the other is doing and a bitter rivalry has ensued. I take breaks because it helps me digest all I have absorbed. Somebody's going to have to shut off the lights. Somebody's going to have to lock the door.

"I want you so bad," I say to another. She's the Her, who must remain nameless because of another. And dirty satyrs with rough faces place bets on the odds of this actually happening the way it has been planned. The rhythm soothes and punctuates the important parts of consciousness. And I begin to realize that it's foolish of me to try and remember the past because what I remember isn't anything like how it happened. Because, like acid, time twists and distorts. And despite the inconsistency, I still love you like I do the moon. My moon. And I hope you don't think I'm trying to pull off your beautifully colored wings.

The weights on my shoulders, and a terrific confusion, is underway. There's nowhere for me to go so I must live HOPE. Maybe one sweet dream will come true for me today like it did for another some thirty years prior to the conception of this improvisation. All images have a STORY. Some images lie like broken glass on the factory floor of life.

Where's home from here? How long can I carry the burdened I've placed upon myself because of my foolish heart? And the theme returns. There is always a tragedy, in the middle of two comedies.

You won't feel so arrogant this time around. Sooner or later I will come to terms with everything and then the world will coldly roll me—punch me in the gut and say good night.

It is here that I will give importance to intention. For cleanliness alone will be our redeemer.

All my children resent me and I've given all my money to the boys up in Duluth. My love's in vain and this repetition is making my heartache. The holes that we used to get sick in are all filled up, so drastic measures must be taken to insure our survival. Now when I speak of HER, it's a different HER, I'm speaking of. So the piano enters slowly but endears us all to the message of failure and all these literary references make me look intelligent but what am I trying to say? All my thoughts are in a knot. The past was walking in front of me the other night, so I blackmailed my better judgment and agreed to have a drink. Intent seems shifty and your righteousness is fraudulent so I'm gonna ride that ol' freight train to a place where your transparent plans can't touch me.

I too have made demands on people in the wrong places and now I'm remembered for telling the future to two lovers on their way to a hanging.

My suitcase is too big for my memories, so I filled it with little stories made up one night with Dr. Juan and a bottle of Wild Turkey. Now the secrets of my soul can be read and passed around and maybe they will instill some sort of secret light into your heart. It's now midnight and everyone knows more than I do and I wonder if the parade went on and are all the streets rejoicing and taking sides? Are all the children armed with flowers, waiting for the parade of their heroes to come by? I just hope it didn't turn into a funeral at dawn. Do I know them? According to your unintelligible letters, yes. Do I care about what they did to that poor old woman and do I care that they tried to have sexual relations with a banjo? No. They're only gonna do it again.

Do all the rings on your fingers mean something? Do all the photographs have a special place in your heart? It's time to start again and I'm not about to let the silly opinions and jealousies of those that surround me have an impact. Now all the street singers are silent and the pedestrians wait with folded arms for their nickel and dime entertainment. So I rub my Utopian lamp listening for a laugh but only hear the scream of spirits coming.

Friends and strangers resign from their positions in life. Lovers call to tell me of their dreams. None of which were true. The mule demands that you open your wrists and let pity begin to flow out and soon the sounds in your head will sigh and fall silent forever.

The specter, that once knelt before me, is now leaving. All this deprivation is leaving dark circles under my eyes. The wine we drink doesn't taste like the wine of the past and this is making me feel bitter towards past and future. Consumption is nothing until the effects make their presence known. Just days ago I lost love because of a lie. Now I sit impotent to action deciding whether or not I should pick up a phone. These names, these names, these names, post no bills on them. And do you hear that sly sound. It's the sound much like the one you hear just before you're about to be mugged or you've already been stabbed in the back and reality is about to set in.

There's a man at the ATM looking suspiciously over his shoulder dreaming of trumped up roles but falling victim to sidewalk spider hallucinations. In the midst of all this poverty and poetry a bluegrass band plays away. I am local traffic, no road is closed to me. I sing odes to lecture halls of past. And I pass the floating head of Jose Marti wishing I had my spectacles and a wall to write on. Alas, nothing is real, so here and there I staple my poems to notices of public intoxication.

Listen up, because one of these days someone important is going to speak their mind. Honest words from a blatantly honest man and tomorrow might be the day I get punched in the mouth. Although blue is the color of despair, I'm still trying to separate her from her underwear—in the romantic tradition of course. And it was a day much like today, that, I, wrote a really bad poem, put someone else's name on it, and made a million dollars. It only works once because all animals will someday eat their young.

The soundtrack for emotion can only be found on vinyl. It will always be misunderstood and true to form of that which be only a pawn. He's a great sun fucker or so I'm told by the slaves of movie houses. And my shoes are full of jewels—diamond rings crown my toes. He is a savior for he has charm in his heart.

If it rains anymore I will speak nothing but honest words. If you continue to stare out of the window waiting for night to come you'll miss out on the boogie-woogie. And like some song of yesterday, one that has great personal significance, life will come back around upon itself, repeating themes, yet now is the time of new understanding, new significance.

Round and round it goes. And the crowd asks, "Who the fuck are you?" You didn't realize that you had walked in with a crown. So you search with sad eyes for a place to sit, a place to feel at home, a place where you will not be disturbed by the thousands of zero's.

And you tell yourself that this is nothing more than the confession of an absurdist trapped in a desire for realism—the continuing struggle that will be set to the music of Charles Mingus.

"How easy is it, to start over again?", I ask you in my most sympathetic voice. "How easy is it, to improve yourself?", You ask, suspicious of my intent. The price of piece of mind has risen significantly since the days of Archibald J. Sunflower.

That's the taste of revolution in your mouth. And it's the smell of revulsion in the air.

Secretly, Sister Psychosis spoke to me today. "Discontentment is all part of the dream, now go and give a history lesson away," she said, never taking her eyes off my boots. So with that I cast a glance and saw the whole picture.

"Never, say never, to the heart of a woman," I said to you. "Never explain yourself to a man who can't tell you how to stop time from going by." You responded, indignantly.

The wooden legged ballerinas and the false grin politicians have settled their differences and Neapolitan ice cream is had by all. Across the street, Virginia Cherrill holds flowers close to her heart. The garden is ready and the chorus of Midnight Dogs and Afternoon Roosters is heard by all and commented on by no one and so I had to ask you, "Does it make anyone happy to hear Bach on the radio?"

BITTER EARTH INITIATES CHAOS AT A LAUNDROMAT

This lagoon is getting too small. No breathing room. In a Felliniesque dream, Picasso lectures me over wedding bread. All my sins are up for discussion. It's getting hard to sleep with present company without feeling that others eyes aren't pressed against the glass.

Everyone knows each other's scent.

It's always the unrecognized genius that gets arrested first. Busted for obscenity and literary fornication. All this falls on blessed shoulders because the wrong questions were asked of the wrong people.

Time later and blocks away, children are splashing in the freezing pool. They're looking for something different. Two are unsure, the other is a new giant. Carelessly they play as Orphan watches on, sipping rum, moaning to himself, "I wish I had parents, they could have taught me to swim." And maybe he's right. But if he wasn't so afraid of his own shadow, his own past, and prematurely ejaculating, he would have someone else teach him.

On a Sunday of self-loathing, I found myself in the company of a man who unconsciously attached Lord to his name. He told me that there was nothing to fear because all the losers in the bar were local and most of them had no interest in my secrets. I asked him, "Are you aware that my secrets run deeper than the filth behind your ears and the three dollars in my pocket?"

On the sly, he informed me, "you had better not mention the three dollars and your hair is too long for a man on a mission."

I lay on a rug, somewhere in the Midwest, clutching a copy of The Weekly World News. All my fellow rebels feel circumstantial pain. Paranoia in on the up and up and everyone in the room is waiting for Homer to open his eyes. He just wants to be left alone with his thoughts, his Playboy, and his cup of tea. The sign on his door reads, *TO LIVE, LOOK LEFT*. Half the people abide. The others find another cause. Some demand their money back. Others still, just sit cross-legged and wait.

The glamorous carry guns and tragic street preachers weep because their universe is coming apart at the seams. There's a docudrama on about professors and all their unpublished books.

The tension in the air is enough to carry us into a more interesting state of mind. And when the lonesome looking gunslinger, whose shirt says Hank on the breast pocket, opens the bar door, the whoosh of air that strikes my face, reminds me of the stale air that fills my nostrils, every time I board a plane.

The walls open, the doors tumble. The songs are falling on deaf ears like machine gun fire. Another village has to be burned in order to replenish the ghosts in your mind.

The moon has been restored to its original splendor and human condition is a story told in two parts.

Was it a simple twist of fate or one too many cups of coffee that lead Hank and I to this moment? This moment that makes history look petty in the eyes of ordinary people. "There are too many names in your prayer cycle—you must discriminate." Hank

informs me. "And is it your impending immuniza-
tion that impedes the Imps from being imperceptive?" I ask. "No," he says eloquently.

There was a time when I thought I had a shot and
being the next Robert Johnson, but neither the
devil nor HER wanted anything to do with me. And
really, who gives a shit about all the why's and
how's of how I reached this point. Sometimes these
are questions that need to be asked and other
times its just best to forget.

Everyone passes slowly, so I reach into their hearts
and plant my seed. It's the tame way to obtain
immortality. Gallantly, my perception restores
disorder and no matter what you say you'll never
understand and now is not the time to lie. My blues
are walking upright as I sink into the white—my
colors rise to the surface leaving a lasting imprint—
proof of my ability to shed lives like dead skin. Each
September grows paler than the last and soon
everything will be transparent. All I want is a love
that sings me to sleep.

The tension mounts and Old Blue Boy has jumped
to sweet paradise. "I can feel my wings sprouting,"

he was heard to shout on the way down. For all I know this is a true story. And for all I know Blue didn't die. He was an American you know. And from a greater height we all shall fall, burn, and rise again. Black replacing blue. But nobody cares about such, unless it involves them or TRUTH is on display. TRUTH is the most misunderstood art form next to the wet dream.

"The wheel will always be in spin," I shouted mockingly at Astronaut Preacher, whose voice cuts like knives. And it was here that I realized that tears will one day replace my grin. And let's face facts, today's Messiahs come multi-colored. The wall between savior and those seeking salvation is thin but impenetrable to those without faith. "Once faith is gone, it's gone," said Charlie Art to Nickel over a cup of tea and carrion. Just then, Lewis Carroll shouted from the bushes, "Desecrate your minds, not holy litanies with your slanderous filth."

There are some that say he's still there because he never had the strength to walk away from that moment in time. Last night I heard my name in a song for the last time. This was also the last time I expressed interest in the good ol' days.

And it was here and now that crimes of passion littered the streets like a ticker tape parade. So, I traded my mind because I knew there would be a better day, not as many stones in my pass-way. And day and night I reinterpret my mistakes in an attempt to find justification. Oblivion is a welcome paradise to what my mind is convinced I've seen.

The old man on his tricycle across the room is as limp and useless as a wet cigarette. It is to him that people write tender poems of confusion and alienation. Tragically, their minds do not oblige them, to thank him for the sheer magnitude of his influence upon my life. He will be forgotten with the passing of time.

Fifteen years ago the glitter factory exploded coating the trials of Hercules in queerness. We were all then forced to yield to the confusion. God's decision making process seemed frighteningly erratic, like a fantasy. But like a bridge it connected the here, now, and soon to be. This is the BIG SECRET!

I have composed 414 love sonnets off the cuff for women and the moon. I wonder which will still proclaim their love in twilight days. Another morning has come and I realize I've got nothing to die for except death itself. And in the midst of all this sadness I learned that I must let all things pass, if I am to become what I am.

I heard a song the other day that sent me back a few degrees to a time when I walked around with gasoline in my back pocket. Knowledge was the only desired power and life's corridor seemed to have a lot more doors. And nothing is as familiar as the unfamiliar forgotten. Dreams, my friend, are the one and only thing that won't let go.

There is something mystical—prophetic—about a flag that leans to the right or left. If it's not parallel to God does it mean that it's not under God? Nothing is as real, as the unreal not realized. The phone rings and I only answer it in my head because there I know what to say—how to feel. But it's okay because there are numerous opportunities in life to be lonely.

"Who is this farmer you speak of who grows Dharma? And why does a hard rain fall on the most precious of souls?" The waitress wouldn't answer.

She has been traumatized by a God that will never take his eyes off of her. In my ear, HER, used to whisper about sweet dreams lost with time, stolen from All The Things You Are. Some of HER scent remains. And my thoughts are thick with love sacred, love profane. The sun has written himself a new anthem in order to relieve us of dead air.

Instead of white noise I let my private psychedelic reel play. And I've filled the cup up with my love without spilling a drop. The cheap thrills over my shoulder only cause me pain.

But I can no longer hide from the light unless I get drunk like I did last night. And on Tuesday I found out that Kid Unconventional failed a test on his own life story. "Details...details," he was heard to have muttered.

I've read the manual and even consulted the cliff notes and I still don't know what to expect in the future. Last night I found hope, in six pack form, and like all else it wasn't free.

That look in your eye says it all. No, I will not forget the things I said even the ones I didn't mean. So let's repeat it all again. All those intricate patterns of love and life. Those double games of the mind. This is what you feed on—this is what keeps those stones in your heart. And there is no answer I can give you without the influence of my own soul. Is it your soul I must take into consideration? My inadequacy to comfort you leaves me feeling hollow inside and even singing the songs I used to sing does nothing but want to make me hide. So I walk into the darkness in order to swallow my pride and admit I knew I would make you cry. And why I never told you this isn't important, because no matter what I say, that bitter taste will always be in your mouth. The rain will always fall upon the mention of my name.

Where there are no "why's" the only word poor Johnny knows is "why". So his dead brother is the only one he speaks to. And a time is gonna come when nights gonna enter his veins and he's gonna want nothing more than to sing to himself.

Three Dog Wonder's older brother, Skip, lectured me on how cold it is where White Night resides. Really, I was only looking for a good time and even though I knew it wasn't here, I stayed because everything else around looked like empty space. And midnight is never permanent unless there are black diamonds in your eyes. And for setting fire to useless beauty I was given a perfect length of rope and a sturdy warning to never play the game. This was the enlightenment I was given. This was my warm gun. And round and round I went until I let it go. Now I need a new coat of paint to go along with my growing collection of marriage, divorce, and motel stories.

I feel a certain sense of boundlessness even though I'm trapped between two images. And I've grown tired of all these Rainy Day Women that surround me. And as I look out into the miles ahead of me I wonder who started the tradition of putting flowers on graves? And who decided apples should be grown in orchards and oranges in groves? I asked a woman at the carnival about this last night, and she looked me in the eye and said, "Screw you and your lifelessness!" I wrote a letter in a moment to myself. And it doesn't matter what it says, only what it intended to say. And it doesn't matter where I'm going, only where I've been. The sun is beating down upon me and I realize that I'm in need of a shave. So many faces passing by me, so many eyes that shine gray. This morning I awoke to the applause of 392 suns.

All the secrets of last night were still fresh in my mind. And how can I fear heights without fearing the depths below. My world is stretching out before me and I have no interest in condensing.

You should have spit out the shards of glass, instead you chewed and swallowed, wallowing in misery. It's nothing but sympathy you speak of as you plot so carefully. And hand in hand we watch buzzards circle historic rooftops where the past ended its misery.

Everywhere about us TRUST JESUS is mysteriously scrawled—an apostle tagging the city in hopes of bringing salvation to all. A true modern prophet? Hobo wino? Performance artist? Nashville? And we sit like ghosts on a bench watching the world go by, stretching strands of mirrors across our fields of play. And no amount of remembering, will make me a child again. And salvation has no saturation point only a letter of authenticity. I've rolled my soul through the muck in order to understand my own disease. And here there are several why's—how's, but no reason for the severity of their crimes.

All those silver rings on your fingers show your obvious guilt. So it must be true that your hiding evidence from the Locals, or your husband, or Elliot Ness. I hired a team of lawyers but it was, Fundamentalist Jive Talkin' Rooster, that kept me out of jail. So out on bail we took a little trip down Drama Lane—where something is always happening and there is no cover charge unless you intend to fall in love. And whether you get it tomorrow or today its always going to be the same. This is the requiem I write for you. This is my congratulations on a job well down. Now I know what it is to be you for forty seconds in a lifetime of forty seconds.

Every scene in my life is a variation of a past scene—an improvisation on a past theme. It's all got me feeling bewildered. As if this is all just a dream. So in the midst of all this you said to me, "The letters now come in droves."

I'm at peace with the fact that I've made no decisions pertaining to whether or not things are the way they are for any other reason than someone has made the decision that this is going to be how its going to be. And outside children are playing games until dawn.

He's been suckered into playing the game again. His famous sister's lawyer from Oregon has seen to it that he'll never again be let out of the maze. And if there is any more rain in his life he might just kill himself. This is how the story goes, this is how the drama is played out. If you see a million people everyday does it mean anything anymore. A prize fighter named Jake once told me, "Sometimes it's just best to take a dive, kid."

And there's no reason for me to think differently— except for HOPE. These new eyes have seen the light.

What is truth but an image conveyed? It's become nothing but feverish disorder. Do you remember the low? The conversation about genealogy? Your rambling lectures on Huck Finn? And in my stoned brilliance I was convinced that it had to do with your obsession with black men. Sullenly, you would roll your eyes and talk about how the Asian Theater was really the only thing that turned you on. "It touches me in a place no boy ever could," you would always whisper with glassy eyes, and school girl grin.

How long is it gonna be, before I let go of the visions of the Promised Land? As clear tears stain clear glass as I watch it all pass by. The numbing agent list is long but none can calm my storm. Swirling, I go to prove myself priest of the invisible.

Each morning as I open my eyes I realize it all means something. All these foolish thoughts that carry weight upon my mind. I tell myself it will all be different two days from now as long as there are two days from now that I will see. And the past is whispering names back at me and in dreams. I see them with different faces. Without contempt I light match after match waiting for Christmas. I sin without regret in order to reduce serious risks to my health. And thoughts that leave the lips haven't the magnitude of those composed and left for dead in the mind.

RKO couldn't TKO a mans vision despite the conviction of another's vision. And all this talk of vision leaves me breathless and without questions. Sadly, the dream continues even though I'm destitute and bored—even with the nightly variables that take place. Sometimes the most revealing things are the ones we can't see. We attempt to pick through the clutter in order to find the important things in life. In the end the juries' always going to be impartial and its imperative that we believe this lie. And is the taste of salvation sweeter than that of condemnation? Is victory sweeter than defeat? It's like ambitious reckless-ness on a Sunday morning goodbye.

The sadness of the events clutches my heart leaving the prose filled with despair. Really, its just one fool telling others his story. An attempt at affirmation, reconciliation, but really there's just a need to be taken home by someone and loved.

They named man SUN in hopes of rising again. And why he never shines they'll never understand. This is the dilemma we've inherited. I've been proclaimed a dreamer, who's needed more when he's awake. It was then that I walked away from the parasitic void, proclaimed myself prophet and inseminator, spoke from the heart and gave what gifts I had.

There's going to be a morning that I'll never see and I know this, just as the rest of you know this. And as

I recall I met a man named Jude Moonlight, and as we sat on a park bench awaiting the inevitable moment when his cigarette burned down to the filter, he said, "Boy, don't try and fight it now, wait until it's right in front of your face."

THE HOBO GOT TOO HIGH AND OTHER ADVENTURES

I'm watching an eight-year-old genius smoke a cigarette and speak of expression. Expression of what you ask? It's fortunate that all dreams end. How could we continue on with life if they didn't? The next night I had another dream and in this dream all eyes were angry but everything felt pure.

Black and white French film rolls before my eyes. Around me the sounds of afternoon groping—lip smacking—zippers undone. A beautiful girl walks into the rest room. Just for a second, I pick my face up off the tile, light rushes to the back of my brain. Face hits tile, the feeling is like a childhood love affair. She's the one wearing white cotton panties with flowers in her hair. The flashbulbs burst, another hooker goes to heaven. And cold morning rain pierces the soul bringing forth concise and clear invocations.

All the masks have fire in their eyes. And I'm beginning to think it doesn't take much more than great tits and ass to be bigger than God. What would Jim Morrison have been without leathers and a pretty face? In the movies it only takes slicked back hair and a five o' clock shadow to look lecherous. But could these actors kill for a loaf of bread? Are you left feeling forgotten and bruised. You were his secret savior and now he must kill you. Just one more kiss before we say good bye.

They are all acts of selfishness. The fire has been lit the funeral planned for the man who played Jesus in a play about Pontious Pilot. And the fact remains that GENIUS always blossoms first as an ugly flower, then a rose, finally a supernova that upon explosion burns the retinas of all mankind.
Everything turns to color when love enters the room. But darkness my children is not far away. And can the giver of wounds heal them? If I remain expressionless will the storm pass me by? Another day passes and I'm knee deep in rum and the past. The stories are flowing out again because I'm in my element and the killer kills with a night light on.

The song feels like a worn grin or a misunderstanding in the moment. It's this series of moments, this series of misunderstandings which causes life to continue on and keep the river of destiny flowing.

Inaccurate recreations on pages, future makes me think again about the passing of time. And the taste is always bitter when you realize that backwards is the direction in which you are moving. My hope is breathing heavily because I can see nothing but the dark heart of crucifixion. So secretly, I make believe that my heart can feel you, but in the end I know you'll be nowhere to be found. And inside, the war is over between Hedonistic Charlie and Methodic Fisherman. And all this my children, is past so I must go the way I want to go, without looking at the other hand. And I sit on cement steps and realize that the world smells like heaven at 3 am.

All the voices speak without hesitancy. And all prophetic journeys should be made on an empty stomach. For there is nothing sweeter than the taste of desire. As it is, there are too many men speaking of waking consciousness. Too many fools waiting for a vision—they want the goods without ever having courted the muse. And I have no time for these deliberate attempts to be shocking. I too can use F U C K free and wild until it don't mean a thing.

I turn my back to the past and repeat my actions with reckless abandon. And again I'm only willing to reveal myself in the darkness. I've looked beyond the places of worship to find the questions that need to be asked but never answered. And every event or action contains the seed of death. It is our obsession to kill what we helped to bring to life. And it is now its duty to give us death with or without a fight. In our minds we bless them with the gift of immortality. They are now actors in mental movies where everything is vague, yet attractive.

We are always leaping from shadow to shadow hoping to find one that fits. Sadly, we always suffer swift injuries do to our naivety. Memories are created from loss. They are our one true coping skill. They play around us like phantoms we cannot touch. They lie in the fine line.

FOUR DIED AND THERE'S A DRUNK GUY ON MY FLOOR

The hat boxes are full of geraniums. The woman, who portrays herself on TV as Scandinavian, is climbing so high, her fall is fatally inevitable. I've met her six times since 8 am and she always acts like we've never met. My thoughtless rowboat, tramp steamer, canoe. My river of thought, birthday salutations and a beautiful drum. Life comes together on a delta refrain. The blue of her eyes has been described as Mediterranean, but she's gone like everything before this.

In tin houses, hurricanes are dreamed, suffocation is the greatest fear. And it's still not me I see in the mirror. There's no pressure in the silence of this room. I try to forget you but you refuse to remain forgotten.

Her Beat book was black and everything about HER face was sunken except for the bones. Tears falling into HER palms. I'll take HER back no matter what she's done.

I've seen love from the bottom of a bottle, through a cloud of marijuana smoke, through translucent LSD eyes. Was there any purity? Any romance?

Leiders and cantos. Two gunslingers make an appointment for dawn. An angel holds the moon in her hand. The lovers remain separated by life. The pain is yet to be realized because they know not of the others touch. Everything falls to the wayside— the muddy puddle on a busy street—the unmarked grave inside my heart.

I sit here, the humidity smothering me, cheap wine passing from lips, to mouth, to throat, to stomach, to brain—trying to make sense of myself and all of my creations. Smoke dangles and slithers around my fingers as I do battle with the swans of contradiction. I don't pick-up the phone because I am a ghost. An impersonator of the man I've convinced others I am. I can't stand the loneliness but I'm on lock down, self-imposed exile, an island of a man. Without a thought I bum a cigarette, knowing that it won't be the last.

I've played the inquisitor with everyone I know, to find out what the reason is for my anger. The intimidation game is being played by all those around me. I can't find the proper speech to dispel all that's rolling within. Thoughts that feel like alibis are pushing me into new depths. Every thing's beginning to feel like an unsure step, a question mark striking my neck.

Salvation is trying to find a void to fill. The timid mule is reveling with his hanger-ons. The Countess, The Duchess, and the Five-Finger Discount Kid are wondering why the Virgins hands are painted gold and why she insists all our roads are wrought with lonely lost souls. After counting every accusation, every inclination, she said, "Every tear feels like a new born sea."

Onward in my journey. Some day's I regret spending the day sipping beer. And every time I lock eyes with you I regret the times you're not there. Circumstance comes on like a freight train. My self-awareness is in a pure state. Words rise in search of a silver lining. I've been here before but the walls were different, the air was noxious, my eyes stung from those white lies. My gaze heads towards heaven looking for the angles riding the storm. And my mind becomes alive as the rough moments begin fleeting. Everybody's talking about having time on the ropes. Something new to fear is only a shadow laden night away. And maybe something is chasing me, trying to get me to remember. The pavement is rolling 'neath me. Ten dollars in my pocket and a night to go.

I've seen the red eyes that wallow and rebel in solitudes filth. A love of madness is the cause of the heart's eternal thump. There's nineteen cents on the ground and my skin feels like sand. Too high to drive or pass an ambition test. High Saint tells me, "That hat makes you look like Whitman." In the corner two French girls make out to the sound of aggressive mambo. I've written exactly 483 poems under the influence of marijuana and I still have not been rewarded with a midget posse.

I can only fuck while listening to Bach's Mass in B Minor. The only words uttered before, during, or after are that of Baudelaire. Across the street from where I scribble these lines, Doctor Nobody is asking for an advance on his soul. And the pageantry of the Bald Skull Fucker has become unwanted.

In dawn light, I imagine cadavers and I imbue colors

rich upon falsehoods. Yet, I haven't enumerated any nations of the soul. And the Alice in my Wonderland is different from yours because my peacock feathers cannot compete with your movie star countenance.

What plagues you most is your hatred for subtle realizations, and the fact that you live your life by the future you find in a cookie. Patiently, I wait for the Fantastic Fool to loose his cool and spill his sins upon the arid ground. And all the books tell me there are ghosts in here. Ghosts whose dreams I steal and make them my own.

Chocolates and the urinals of Marcel Duchamp remind me of the fact that there will always be another bender—always be a dream for the dreamer. I chose the abstract to represent reality. I pray to Goddess Moon instead of God Sun and still people turn and laugh at me even though I've made no solid declarations.

Will it be this train that will be my grave? The spirit leaves us in a blink. And I want art to be as sexless as hydrogen. Ambiguity. This poem has no cunt or cock. Now is the time when a multitude of angels dance in the palm of my hand. And your eyes lament moments that began but never ended. I came for the rum and left with self oblivion and a girl on my arm. In haste I burned all my poems and sprinkled their ashes off bridges and causeways into the waters that gave them initial life and again they shall have life.

IMAGINATION speaks to me and as a result I fill the air with carbon monoxide.

Tonight, I've given all the entertainment I can give so I turn on the TV for the first time in six weeks and my consciousness is altered and deranged more so than any acid ever could.

I've seen the house of a thousand fine days and in its yard I planted my flag, posted a sign proclaiming my lust for life. I am obsessed with the pressure placed upon fictional characters. The voice on the other end of the line brings back a heartless dream. An exercise in romanticism. All things come to pass.

SANCHO PANZA AND LADY DAY

Velvet monkeys in euphoria trees shout at the ghost of the sun. In time all our bodies will be crushed by a thunderous blow from the feather of ecstasy. And this meaningless blow will resound through the universe until the last tree that no one heard fall comes tumbling down.

The natives have grown silent. So with this kiss you will never be lonely but you will never again be adored. Now is the time that all your thoughts turn to the games that you've played and all your distant memories come back to haunt you with bitter distinction. All those pools of thought that we try to submerge ourselves in without drowning are really, just knee deep. And all the scenes are defined as hip and it's been four long years since I've seen the shining, angelic face of Nashville. But the rumor is, he still wanders those lonely streets with the jack o' spades in his shirt pocket.

My state of mind has become overgrown—my paper crown ripped off my head and I find myself foolishly looking to the future. Waiting to watch it go by—

flaming on the river—a death raft piercing our minds. Our mornings are no longer velvet. Days are lived in dreams, nights reserved for sweet debauchery.

God has reinvented sex because disease fell upon him as it did us and what is valuable to the sidewalk dancer is of no meaning to the man on the bus that always asks, "What world is that?" And 3x3 women transfuse blues upon an immune soul of candy-corn joyride. We must find in what way we all wish to be compulsive. The boys and girls who grow up to star in porn can see the light at the end of the tunnel.

"The Gibberish falls neatly in standard rows." The defendant said to the Judge, which in this case was the towns only nurse.

The sink barks at me and the power sockets spit invisible fire. I scream Ozymandias in their direction but their reply is always grim. And time moves quicker than we'll ever realize.

SCREWING THE POLAR BEAR FOR FREE

The cosmos no longer vibrates—it quietly hums like electronic impulses.

Everyone here smells like soap or the ashy deposit at the bottom of the soul. Feelings become concise in the haze of marijuana and neon lights. The street moves and I stay still.

Rain beats upon my windshield—streaks into the unknown. Nothing but darkness ahead and my mind is plagued by HER face. A warm sensation fills my brain every time I look down at HER picture. The world seems to drop and I'm left on a street corner with a beer in my hand cursing at a bus stop bench. Then a six fingered man passes by and asks me about adventure. Not knowing whether this is an invitation or not, I decline saying, "I just don't have the spirit for it any more." I blink and the sun's up. Time's been lost again—never to be found—never to be heard from.

Another day in the life of the crew of the Rocketship Crucifix. The dirty bastard's wings have been clipped and all their songs are being sung by others to their lovers. And somewhere a little girl has just found her hand in the confusing mess of cotton sleeves. I turn away in despair and for the first time I noticed that all the posters are telling me to vote independent and all the electric chairs are hungry for flesh and all of Texas waits in anticipation for that smell of cooked flesh.

What machine killed Woody Guthrie? Was it a suitcase full of razor blades? Was it natural selection?

A legion of pondering fools contemplates the new religion without taking into consideration INEVITA-BILITY.

I walk around like some late night psychopath waiting for a sign. The sun comes up and I return to normal again. Like the rabbit being chased at the greyhound track. Yes, good man, I know what it means to lie. And yes, I can smell the stench of Apocalypse on your clothes.

What holy harmonies transcend time and space granting us epiphanies? With great heights of mind, I stare down the eyes that come without thoughts, that repeat a series of actions in order for me to write in detail their history. Great knowledge gained, but what's the loss? Where's the independence in thy eyes?

It's a brand-new time but the words used to describe it are those of similarity. And it is those, outside this place, that are mad. They have purity in their eyes. It was Wallace Stevens who said, THE PHILOSOPHER PROVES THE PHILOSOPHER EXISTS. THE POET MERELY ENJOYS EXISTENCE.

COLDER THAN A WELL-DIGGER'S ASS

"My blind faith in the muse is what has been getting me to sleep at night."

I remember the night you uttered those words that touched me so sweetly like a brick to the nose.

Foolishly, I told you all about my dreams last night and you laughed at my despair. Once I saw you in my clouded heart and I realized there was nothing equivalent to this.

My enemies are getting uglier with time and I've butchered all the past catch phrases I could. The palm tree tops blow in the angry breeze of a hurricane that will again pass as a black widow crawls across my face looking for an entrance into my electric brain.

Every day for decades I used to write letters to the man I was told handed out happiness asking him for a bit. He just sent me stained and malformed geometric puzzles.

There are 420 degrees of pronunciation and we'll always be left to wander about the strange man of last week. Our commissioned heroes have returned for their tulips and they ask repeatedly about the distinct smell of rose that fills their heads every time they say your name.

The 44 came after 19 and that was a time long forgotten by the stuttering bums of old 13th Street. All the clues are revealed about a life without much appeal. And when will Nashville resurrect himself? The legions of followers are waiting.

Pantheistic innovations and they got the mongrels on a spit. She tells me the pink pills make the voices go away and in the storm clouds my mind drifts. Here's the place where the faces are oh so pale and there's too much blood on the pavement to see the trail of tears. And tonight the prophecy must be fulfilled—I must be what I never wanted to be—I must now think about the times I might have had, had I never opened my mind to Blake's light. How does one respond to a straw crowned queen? She waves me away and the horizon runs red and black. It's all just another day to die and a train leaves every half hour.

My ambitions are phantasmal and I watch virgins sleep, feeling their thighs for the moistness left from innocent dreams. Like them I am consumed with the unknown.

NASHVILLE AND THE HURT

The sight of dead roses can't stop my thoughts from swaying with the days. And here and there we all get a glimpse of heaven but never a brighter day. The front porch of a drunk is hung on the wall in front of me, and advice is being given freely on the fine art of giving a lap dance to the legless super-heroes that were wounded by good intentions.

I go looking again, for the already been, and I'm left standing alone. In the park the rain's falling and Sister Lover has a nose full of coke. And this bald man is rejoicing because of the lack of rules in the game. Sixteen times a day and in 79 different ways, I unleash my unexpected madness without regret.

The best kisses are stolen and the best resurrections are at hand. My windows are beginning to reflect and the moon begins its descent. I've had all the fun I'm allowed to exhuming the dead. All the commercials are running together and forming patterns of orange, leaving us with a feeling that's something like centripetal force or a punch in the mouth. And the back door has closed on the night—the lonely spider crawls down the wall and eternity flashes before me like a supernova.

The traffic is raging outside yet the dust has settled and I can't keep my hands off the breasts of the 80 yr old woman that's sitting next to me in the theater. Citizen Kane is playing and I know I must hurriedly get out because it all feels like pornography in here.

I walked into a rest room where a girl was giving a stubby-dicked motherfucker a hand-job. They watched themselves in the cracked mirror. When I walked in, they screamed.

I told them I had to take a piss. She began to cry so I pissed on their shoes. When I walked out, I watched two lesbians pour water down each others shirts, I asked them if they knew Nashville. "Sunday's two days away," they said in unison.

The longer this play continues the sadder the boy with chubby hands gets. He's a big zero, a man dependent upon his teenage angst to get him through. The older he gets, the longer it takes him to get an erection and soon it will take him 16 hours to even feel it.

A strange German girl tells me the kids call him Impotent Billy, fighter of the good fight.

Wanda comes into the room with a picture of Nashville in Quebec and goes into a rant about blotter acid and necrophilia. "Which is more powerful?" I asked her with true interest.

"You have too many cadavers on your floor," she comments, part in bitterness, part in hesitation. I forgive her, she's got a diseased cunt that all the boys from uptown want. She says it's from pesticides but I know John Henry drove in his death spike and now the eternal hatred has begun.

The Cains who need no Abels. The victims of a war within themselves. The ones that notice the dishonesty of their world when it is viewed in the moonlight.

Between you and I, I am looking for a place to go—another roof to cover my head.

More dreams to leave unfulfilled.

It's AB followed by STRACT.

Outside black smoke billows from where a star fell to earth and caused the fall of an empire and I watch it all from behind a pair of dark shades. In the kitchen, I mix paint in various Campbell Soup cans and I'm instantly transformed. Instantly, I shed a tear and find myself high.

The rubber cement sniffed, brought back a flood of memories. From the back of my head to the front, old movies replay.

The room is filled with bare skulls and they all are wondering if there is a porn star alive that doesn't have acne on her ass. The cold that comes in from the outside brings us back to the moment of birth. Being ripped from the womb and placed on the front lines of a nasty and endless war.

Kindness Is a Stripper That Makes Change.

ADVENTURES IN
THE FALSE MIRROR

In the softness of the afternoon, with heavy eyes, those thoughts come back 'round.

Struggling with you and those reflecting images. I've made a new start with a new heart. That trackless train running through my weary head. And out from Grandma's eyes comes confrontation. Somewhere, in the lonely night, Billy the Kid, is resting his bones as Hypocrite and Hooker come walking down my street. They're just passing the time talking, because there's nothing left to feel. And what's with all these realizations, this desperation, this falling in love with the drama portrayed by silly incest casualties. The man who works behind the counter at the liquor store is looking for a fight or someone to share his stories with. He's on an insatiable crusade.

Sometimes things have to be hands-on. In the air there is a sense of celebration. The outlaw's been out for one month out of the last eighteen. He's drinking and feeling the fate of the opossum. Staggering, staggering, staggering away with a little envy in me. Why must my life be so damn strange?

Too much desire in the veins of my fragmented self. The runner had two lovers on the side. I'm watching him as I stand in a moment. Stand in an absurdist, nineteenth century French Quarter. Drunkards, clowns, girls with promises fill my eyes and I make fate a deal, if she'll just listen to my strange demands, as I pass wicked eyes and flaming iron arms. It's to her I talk most of the night, and yet I'm convinced she doesn't even know my name.

Waking up, feeling like I've been swallowed whole. Three in the afternoon. I'm staring into the grains of an old picture frame. The houses on the mountainside all possess rattlesnakes who know my name.

Flim-flaming the perspective. Battling for direction. What's become of the fingerprints you left on my skin and brain? Trying to turn back the water that's rising high as childhood dreams fade away. Reciting commandments like careless replies. The bitter tongue that had once turned your head now leads me around another corner, down another street, to the front of another door.

Resting myself in the song I sing when thinking of you. A saint, a piano player, and a well rested Billy the Kid ride through the town of Coincidence. I was sitting tall, in an IHOP, listening to Tribal Chief laugh about white men's wives tales. And as I close my eyes I watch the sun mingle with your eyes and I disguise myself as some kind of joke.

Cashing in on the dreams that hung above like stars on a string. The enchanted snakes are busy drinking away their gloom—their kisses are dark and cause suffocation. And my rueful language is leaving the taste of mothballs in my mouth. My tired eyes, again, have let me down in my quest to SEE. And I never let myself get cut 'cause I bleed too fast. A long tall gentleman once told me a story of which the moral was, it's all about your stride not your gyration. The bluntness of your instrument has everything to do with its effectiveness. And it's not on this road that I'm addressing.

Knee deep in a funny shade of blue. The picture frame is crooked and broken. Jesus sits in all four corners of the room and the woman that fears him sits reading a poem I wrote for her. She tells me she loves me just the same.

Feeling salvation in my weary bones is a thing of the past. Like dinner in lines and walking around in a cowboy hat.

Being manipulated by circus commercials. The smoke dances through the winter air with graceful sorrow. The whispers mix with your kisses and laughs. Metaphors for life support. Faith elects to resign. Guilt is irrelevant. No words tell what is true.

The Catholics are advertising on late night TV. 1:31, a train whistle blows. It's all done for adulation. A bigger crown for someone to steal.

All the boys sing a tune in general population, except for Rodeo Clown and Payphone Sam. They've got no friends to see them through. It's been said that their visions are platonic and their egos are the size of a light turned off.

Headlights. Drunk, like the days I roamed the streets like a hummingbird. Every few steps I punch a man with a cigar in the throat then fuck his girlfriend, filling her with my memories, that they would unknowingly lick out when they came to.

The progress of jazz and dirt. Life given to my bamboo chutes. The cheap wine is being emptied by the sadness that lives in me. And I've fallen for the girl, who has fallen for the midgets. There was a gun at the party and I was tempted to put it to my head and empty it until the world knew how dirty my pact with the devil was.

NIGHT OF THE SILVER-TONGUED MACHIAVELLIANS

Suicide done artistically. Brains splattered on the floor. Reminded of Pollack's paintings. The violins come in and all the school children turn the other way. No harm done—the dreams fall just like they did a day, week, year ago—their ashes find a place in the void.

In the other room the TV hums and I realize there's nothing left to see. Naturally I will dream an ending to this short film about the floating going-ons of desire. Is it LOVE or escape we're really feeling, dreaming, romanticizing?

Visions of a hunchback running for president. "Aqualung" his campaign song. And I ask him if ignorance is getting free form and is technology rhapsodizing on the shoulder of Psychopathic Ingrate.

Whose magnanimity is in question? Whose suffering has been rejected do to lack of contrition? The tone is mesmerizing to the born insane. My troubles will reside in an hour.

Someday completeness will set in. The alarms will resound. The creation of something to believe in, underway. And they no longer want your love but something sacred. And all the new letters begin with "You know".

Dreamily, my skepticism begins to rise until my throats filled and my eyes show nothing but underage darkness.

Is this all an unbearable declaration. The cool, light a fire. And the drummer with gravy spoons finds his time.

Slow to progress. Quick to undress. Love burns like a funeral pyre. But even that will be out marched by death.

All truth slips away. Drifts. Never to be seen the same way again.

Pestilence and penance. There's a glimmer of hope in the eyes of someone that's made to squirm. And the rain just drips on my head as I begin to think about all those that have left or affected me.

Heads heavy with drunken hypnotism. I possess every word and gently they rise and dance before my eyes.

Sensory deprivation, sensory explosion, both feel like a thousand tiny spiders crawling across my back. It's restraint minus harmony.

Reject the art because it lacks passion. The only tear I ever shed has long since washed away. And still Death nor a Lion are waiting to enter my room. So like Judas of old I will find a scapegoat, a martyr, a condemned, a child of Fate.

Antagonist Behemoth, shoves but never throws a punch, even though he has nightly wet dreams about showing off his might. And the vision has become a wisp just as visions of Nashville have become faded like drawings of roses in charcoal.

It's been 21 years since I last dreamt of a sunrise. Nothing but sunsets or mystical flashes of light. And for the last six nights the tower has toppled down upon me.

The eye strays. Plays the game that it must. I smear stars across the midnight sky like blood on a belly of wheat.

I gave birth under blue light. The heavens above looked like a cluster fuck of God eyes. No more good can be done.

The music grooves in backward motion. Feels like one of Billy's time jaunts. No more delusions—no more passivism—no more hands for me to hold.

Blind men cackle and shout out discolored memories and wish for brown Mississippi River dreams. And I'm waiting to see the black eyes of Allen Ginsberg in the light of day.

Is it atrophy or the primal beast in me that claws from the inside out causing blood to trickle from my nose and mouth? Doors are locking—sighs are being let out. 20 seconds takes an hour. I look for my niche in one of the many sides of paradise.

The dawn enters stage right. I continue to be hunted by the name I once proclaimed.

Watching over my shoulder as I cross the streets, I've crossed a thousand times before.

Tears now have different colors and vowels. She tastes of turpentine and Florida which makes me want to do nothing but sleep.

One never knows what he will remember in the end. So next time you see Nashville, spare a dime— ask no questions—search for no resolution.

Bits of revelation are picked from between the teeth of the already fattened and are traded to the starving masses for their souls.

Fingers move like dancing spiders on my window ledge. Pace and pulse, quicken.

Each note is from and for the soul.

I see words engraved on the inside of my skull.

The moon still longs for the return of jazz high nights. Watching BIRD wail from rooftops. Young POETS, first time high, staring out of their windows into her misanthropic eyes.

There's a hole of expectation to fill. A voice in my head that I need to question about its presence. Then decide if the firing squad should be called in.

The most tragic events lacerate us for years to come until the taste of BLOOD is potent in the back of our throats. And it is here that rain and vomit mix in the street. In and Out of Consciousness. I dance Above Fire.

FINNEGAN BENDS TIME AND OTHER STORIES

What is it that follows sunshine? A change in features? Where does it go when it's all gone wrong? Sweet Sally got remixed by the Kleptomaniac's disease. And we're all waiting for Queen Edie's return. It's practicality and speed. It's crying all night and buying a drink for each tear. It's a song with too many words. It's a dream with too many metaphors. It's the one that's too hard to follow. It's for all the pin-up boys and girls everywhere. It's just a little something that will kill you fair and square.

I'm just trying to recapture that feeling I had while I was getting blown for the first time.

It's again too much. All the names look like toothpicks in a box. The nausea is rising against me. I'm being hunted down by balding Euro-Thrash that carry communist leaflets in their back pockets. I've been stealing water from the veins of anyone I come across for weeks.

I am no better or worse than anyone else—it just appears that way in the light of day.

Our modern heroin is being cut with the ashes of junkies past. We still haven't any idea who our angel of revolution is or where to look. Maybe more time is needed. Fear needs to be buried deeper. Each side is raising their electric fists and shouting for a redeemer. I glance left than right and look for the rocket's rise and penetration of imaginary universes. And do these poems ever reach conclusion or do they blend into the next life.

Poor John's dream rolls off our tongues like symbolic numbers. Maybe all he's saying is that he's tired of dirty lonely sheets—tired of the bus to heaven being broken down—tired of the TV that is a metaphor for suicide or redemption.

The child has grown up but he still dreams. His eyes carry that subtle brilliance as he walks down sidewalks. The shadow of Nashville right beside. And this song, brings back memories, quiet nights, 1930's Depression era parlors, no hope insight. A flash—memories of rainy Atlanta city streets—a bloodied drunk crawls to heaven' s door. "His ambition died when America let God die," is what Madame Rose declared as the reason for any misfortune.

The voices in her head have begun to layer—it's all beginning to sound like guttural Dutch. And the Emperor's tomato soup is burning on a transients hot plate. The hot dogs are cooking on hot irons and Blue Rimbaud has nowhere else to go. And behind Lightin' the sign reads RABBITS. And the newspaper reads, ACCORDION RELATED CRIMES ARE ON THE UP & UP.

Wish me luck on finding a safe haven from all this abuse. A place to hide from all the useless talk that's circling my head in furious fashion. My wings are soiled and I've crashed to the ground.

In blue-green-yellow river dreams the violins are silent, the army trudges forward and the birds sing a different, more profound song.

Schools of thought have been split, and Nashville's in need of a new pair of shoes. His girls got California eyes, a Nevada chin, and a heart...Well, she's got a heart without boundaries.

Does the flower KNOW perfection? Does the minute KNOW it's part of an hour? Does the color KNOW it represents a vowel?

The sun shines and the church still decays as I decay as the movie house decays. It's a way out we seek but a means of conquering is what we want. There was a time prior when I had so many more expectations, a time when I thought I'd see forever and a day. Situations being what they are and I being who I am...

Why is death the remedy we all dream of? Is there something tender about its inescapable grasp?

The secrecy is sworn. The randomness of the goals forgiven for the sake. The inexplicableness of all that has been said? Is this really random or previously thought out?

HOBO GHOST TRAIN

How will it end? How will the world look at me in a time after now? The whiskey's lost its taste. Everyone around is asleep. I'm a red-eyed apprentice to ghosts. In my mind, stand bedeviled figures. Raw nerved poets with calloused hands, raspy howling voices that can invoke God and the devil in one moan.

There are rumors and fables being spread about you and your anger towards the world. What do you have to be so angry about anyway?

The moon is hiding itself and already I can hear your tired tears on the other end of my phone. Nothing but boredom and separation are where caring and concern once were.

Your vicious cycles don't do anyone any good. I'm looking to get away from this alcohol suffocation and you again are the willing fool.

The circus is in town and you no longer have any ground to stand on. You are as thin as a cloud, just like my Uncle Felix's wife. Not even enough strength to kill yourself. Who am I to say a word? Who am I to stop you from plunging your self into desolate seas? You've learned nothing from the hours that have passed, or do you just like the sight of your own blood. No longer will I allow you on my leather couch. Find a new ear, a new shoulder, bury your hypocrisy in the dark ground. Your sadness is a drama played out to keep us all near.

Too much dirt in my mouth to fall from here. The restlessness has a direction and an angel winks at me through the trees. And I know that when I get too high there's someone out there to grab my heels 'cause the moon told me so. In the distance thunder rolls like chimes of freedom. And it all appears like a dream— fragments—only the important pieces remain.

In this theater of loneliness and desperation I've been told that I am Shakespeare's other brother. And all the fruit from my trees, along with the poisoned squirrels are on the ground.

I'm walking down the street that runs the length of the world. I was struck by the neon and the desolate sleeping. The sirens wailed, the guitar player, for a change, was murdered.

Fantasies come with the prostitutes, who all have bad livers and broken hearts and pray to no one to fix it. The lions run in a field that was never before theirs. And everyone's vying for company and the key of release or a mass written for them.

The images before my eyes remind me of a frighteningly beautiful woman I once knew. She is now broken, but keeps herself together

In her clothes. She is a novel without an ending. The best I can say is that she opened all the doors. Opened them wide, smiled, then leapt through the mirror, into another world I wasn't aware of.

I've been offered rainbows but the rain's always falling. I've heard the song that answers all the questions and found that no one was listening. It's those same people that wonder why they're so empty.

The frail fraudulence of life. Dali dancing in sharp surrealist light. The cherubs utter words of melancholic nature. Expressionist Monk dances with the drunks. A child sleeps in the thick of it.

The SOHO Kid went in like Starsky and came out like a young Brando. A sign of the times in the city of priests and industrialists. In this shaky Black Velvet morning, I realize that the enemy of my enemy is deeply rooted within myself. And as I stand in the sand that I've stood in a thousand mornings before, I rejoice in the fact that I am not the man they think I am.

MIDNIGHT THOUGHTS OF THE MEXICAN SUN

Afternoon sun blasts into the room of socks and shoes. There's no one below giving out rainbows. In a few hours the rain's gonna start falling and I'm not gonna want to leave the house. All the souls outside will be forgotten. No use in wondering why this all takes place.

The vast cast of characters from the past never figured it out. Why do you think you or I will?

Go back to your front porch, your dreams and restless rest. I'll remain here listening for trains and ghost glory.

The desperation of freedom moans like a sad harmonica. The feeling is released slow and easy. The lion emits, lover forgives, a back is never again turned. Sun sinks, water splashes, the high takes it to another place. There's so much beauty out there that I'll never see, never touch. Eyes and hands to callous to let it in.

There are no sins to recant. No lover to dismiss. No dream to remain unfulfilled.

Reality buzzes like a radio that can never be tuned. I've been to her room, but from out her window I couldn't see the moon. The guards have left their post— the room is filled with smoke. The Minotaur gets silly, the President whispers, "Too much coke." Needless to say, they got sent back to where they came from. Invisible ticks eat holes into my legs. My hands are tied to the sanity pole. 20,000 leagues from here, a 5th symphony is discovered for the first time. The composer was buried in another man's shroud.

Is time measured in silence? Pain, a choir of angels singing? I hear no bells chime though I know it's midnight outside. The bricks before your eyes, the wall collage, the poetry and disease will tell a story you haven't realized you've been told.

The love sickness of America. There is no hour too dark to leave this paradise, this is the moment of Judas' absolution.

Defying fate, I choose not to sleep on nights like tonight.

Is death still courting poetry? Has he gotten her goods? Sodomy and all?

I hear no voices on the other side of the line, just the gagging sound of those choking on Van Gogh's ear. Does madness even have a sensation anymore? Has bad drinking water ever tried to seduce you? Right now there's a song playing for you. Creation and rhyme unfold. I think about lost Saturday afternoons of lazy TV and swift rain. Every time Bearded Elliot enters the twisting room the locals ask if he has a story to tell. He just repeats the sounds he heard on the walk over. A requiem for a smile that wore a man.

A bundle in a back pack. God hides in the dark. The Devil hides behind the gate. The delivery boy's face has been bitten by Death but he has nothing to fear. His hand contains a jack and an ace. Still, he realizes there's a sadness in the passing of time, sunsets, moon rises, the shadow like the tooth grows long. Angels appear before us like smoke. The empty-handed conquerors illuminate, then pass like dust. The dead have left on runaway trains. The old men from three towns away have come to steal your shoes. Somehow this song just passes through.

Everyone loves a man who can make them laugh and abuse himself with one clever line. The coffee has gotten cold, the butter soft, the eggs huddle together, the body breathes its last breath.

The light flickers. A head turns to dust. A piano plays softly. The light breaks off the edge. Flowing shadow. Elegance in azure.

The lover's lips tremble with the first kiss. How much longer can they wish on the same simple star?

The million-eyed monster has risen up in order to typify our current state. Countless years, spent, with face on the pavement. And what are the proper manners when two lovers converge in a lake? The corners of the clowns mouth are cracked, but the picture is perfect.

Are there too many murders on television? Are the quacks just out to make a buck?

Are the painters pockets full of self-assurance? Has Hades grown too strong? Are the other gods on bended-knee? Can sight come from the seen?

If you cannot understand why the mirror is unreasonable, try the window. Tragedy swirls in the eye of the universe. Poetry is the unexpected thing. The vicious rabbit that sinks it's teeth into the soft-bodied fawn. Compliments are given, bare breasts touched. The exchange of pain filled words with the face in a lonely window.

I weep over the wind and the acts I have committed. I weep over my compliance, my reaction to Ophelia's tortured response. I weep to the sounds of gypsy hymns. The old soldiers beg for flowers and Gods mercy—the rest of the world is silent. An hour later I hear nothing but my foot steps resound down the empty paths of this sterile field.

Today, maybe another day, another saint, I whisper into the ashes of childhood to find the answers.

Suspiciously they wink, dressed in bloodied wedding gowns. Snakes slither across their chests.

It was all a dream about childhood religious experiences. Ink drawn hallucinations are all that remain.

Twisted iron and hunks of flesh. Pristine snow covering a field. Somewhere there's a war going on. Somewhere love is being made. Everywhere a dreamer dwells. This abyss feels like the air trapped in my fist.

The roll of dice in the tomb of golden bones. Memories of mighty splendor. We are all imitations of mental inflictions. Too foolish to see the light. Heart of paper, soaked by rain, destroyed before I even got to your front door. A temple with no sex, is no temple at all.

IN OBSERVANCE OF MEMORY AND DREAM

A man with a renewed sense of vigor stands in sin shoes with broken heels, tips his hat to the lady passing, she smiles back wishing her husband was dead. The day progresses like a broken watch.

The river's to my neck and rising. Too many reasons now for the girl not to return my phone calls. Stoned and vacant hearted, a longing that won't let go. I pass the time that's moving painfully slow. She is amongst the wild flowers and I lie with the haunted roses, striving for a higher place, striving to open myself up. Reaching for the moment that I can feel love in my veins.

Engaging Pilate in a game of gravity. No age has succeeded in escaping the grasp of doctrine. They begin to drown at birth. And I'm lost in the rain, thinking about your soft eyelids in the moment of love. Feeling visceral and head-long. There's a presence in the room that defies color.

The mountains have met the poem, together they contemplate the cross and the humble flesh that's born from the fruit, like an eternal blossoming rose in the hand's palm.

The traffic breaks as I pass-bye the old apartment of the woman I lost because of a lie. Outside her front door Eternal Custer and Achilles shake to their partnership over a sleeping bum's eyes.

Picasso's geometric flesh makes me cry. Breathing in the shadows of certain towns.

Hearing Beethoven's triumphant call at Death's door. Star-shaped, the lady in waiting, brought a blind man to the party. The booze loosened his tongue and then he turned into a ghost.

Carry the world's weight upon a single shoulder and I will no longer weave lies or scratch graffiti upon your heart. Let me be silent for just an hour. Let me fade.

It's all over when Laughing Man dies. And I go nowhere without a tear-stained rosary in my pocket. By the sweat on your brow and the expression on your face I can tell your story is much like my own. The voices are down to a whisper and the night has come to a tired end.

And we step out into the dawn like weather-beaten children. The day, like the night, has a thousand eyes.

All the debts have been paid, yet you're still in chains. I've realized 510 different ways to sell one's soul. And all those junkies look into the moon only to see the sun. An old man walks the streets selling dictionaries and in desperation you buy one and try to learn all the words that you already know.

The sound of rain gently falling. The smell of a burning cigarette. This is what I awake to. This is what I dream in moments of soft sleep.

The blind judge has ordered the hanging of the pencil drawn man and the crowd responds with apathy. The violin player with skeletal countenance weeps at the realization of his dark beauty. The poet weeps because he is a witness. And the only act I've witnessed was the street singer opening her heart.

Which are the memories that the mind conjures up as being the sweetest? Do they include the brilliance of infinite stars? Maybe just the light of someone's eye? A candle flickers. I catch the soft wax in the palm of my hand in order to seal the stigmata.

Seeing is believing and no one can deny me that.

There's never an end to a life bitter spent. The dream comes on like a come down and now it's all just images passing before my eyes.

The hobo obituaries are posted in the courtyard. My face is on fire as the past calls me to the front. Seduced by whiskey and the moon, I moved inside you and felt that feeling I thought had died.

Alas, this light, this darkness, is no more mine, than it is yours.

The blind boy crashes into the SIGN. His brother drops his games and slaps him across the back of the head. He does it because he's never been the favorite, the loved. He is the only one that can tell the difference between the blind man and the one who just doesn't see.

Patterns. Consciousness malformed like ellipses. It's all gone back out to sea. The past has returned in vain.

Horrified mornings. Afternoons that slip by. An adrenaline rush brought on by the falling sun. The senses stimulated, then deprived.

The trouble comes just as I forget that Nashville and Death are in a neck and neck race to my door. Which one will lose their will? Their power?

Their heart?

My seeds of distinction have grown into beautiful flowers that attract the most vile.

The most innocent.

No thorns.

No blood loss.

The final possible moment has arrived. I see YOU.

HER.

HER AND YOU.

One in the same breath.

My madhouse acquaintance that talks rapidly of
revolt. YOU who broke YOUR foot trying to kick
through the invisible, pissed YOURSELF, put
curses on the heads of your captures, succumbed,
still screaming with blood running from your ears.

I shed midnight fears for I am a man striving to steal
all he's seen.

Forced back into the eye, through the mind, shot
into the heavens, and back into flesh.

Printed in the United States
119812LV00002B/56/P